T0375544

A DREAMER'S DIARY

A DREAMER'S DIARY

DETHRONING THE UNDERACHIEVER

TIM JONES,
THE MOTIVATIONAL POET

COPYRIGHT © 2008 BY TIM JONES, THE MOTIVATIONAL POET.

ISBN: HARDCOVER 978-1-4257-6878-2
SOFTCOVER 978-1-4257-6854-6

All rights reserved

Reproduction of this publication in any form or by any means is strictly prohibited without the expressed consent and prior written permission of the author.

This book was printed in the United States of America.

Write:

Motivational Poet
4147 White Heron Drive
Orlando, FL 32808
mopoet@juno.com
www.motivationalpoet.com

To order additional copies of this book, contact:
Xlibris Corporation
1-888-795-4274
www.Xlibris.com
Orders@Xlibris.com
37768

Contents

Dedication

This book is dedicated, as always, first and foremost, to GOD, my Father, who has given me life, the passion to live it, and the determination to live it to its fullest! Secondly, it is to my wonderful and beautiful wife, Regina, who is all 'the woman' I will ever need. Thirdly, it is to our gifted children, Kemuel, Jewel, and Harmonee, who are constant reminders of why my struggles must become my weapons of victory. Fourthly, it is to all the dreamers who are not afraid to pursue their dreams passionately. Keep on pressing on. For though the vision tarries, wait for it! It will surely come!

And finally it is to those of you who are afraid . . . .

WAKE UP BEFORE YOU DIE!

Author's Note

Hello, my name is Tim Jones and I am the Motivational Poet. I want to first of all thank you for acquiring this book and taking the time to read it. I don't take it lightly that you have decided to give ear to what I have to say. I am a devoted husband to my one wife and a committed father to my three children. I was raised in a small town in Georgia by parents who taught me to serve God, respect my elders, love my enemies, work hard, and believe in myself. I grew up believing that I had something inside of me that would change the world. I still believe that today. Only now, I believe that everyone has something inside of him or her that can change the world.

You know, there is something very special about you. You were created to do something unique in your time and space. Do you know what that is? Most people don't. Many have set goals and reached them, dreamed dreams and achieved them only to find life yet withholding its substance. This is because success, as we know it, is not life's goal; fulfillment, however, is. The substance of life is found only in the purpose of life or, more exactly, the fulfilling of that purpose. That's why it is essential to know the purpose for your life. You must have something to live for so that when you die you don't die for nothing. I believe that every person is born with a rhythm in their soul, a dream in their heart, and a triumph in their spirit. I also believe that when you find the rhythm for your life, it will expose your dream, lead you to your purpose, and bring you to your destiny!

It is interesting to note that there is a unique connection between what you really want to do with you life and what you were created to do; what you really want from your life and what you were born to have; what you really want to be and what you were destined to become. You must realize that you do indeed have something inside of you that can change the world. It is your dream! But in order for your dream to change the world, you must realize it. In order for you to realize it, you must pursue it. In order for you to pursue it, you must embrace it. In order for you to embrace it, you must acknowledge its birth within you. That's what 'A Dreamers Diary' is all about—the birth, pursuit, and realization of the dream.

Introduction

"When you were born the plan was not that you should fail, but that you would succeed. It was not that your life should be worthless, but that it would be worthwhile. It was not intended for you to have a negative impact on the world, but a positive one. It was not meant for you to have less than the best, but the very best life has to offer. You were predestined in love to succeed before the world began. That means that the destiny for your life was determined before you were born and the decision as to where you should end up and what you would become was not a toss in a hat, but a well thought-out plan to bring you to the full manifestation of expressed love through the maximized potential of your predetermined purpose."

If you are reading this book, you are doing so because you were drawn by the title, design, colors, or maybe even someone's recommendation. It is, however, most likely that you were drawn by the part of you that knows no barriers, cannot be broken, will not be dominated, and always triumphs—the part of you that was designed to win, hit the mark, accomplish the task, make the goal, achieve in every thing you do. If you are not experiencing a satisfying level of personal success and achievement in every area of your life, it is, no doubt, due to the underachiever within you.

Who or what is the underachiever?

The underachiever serves as an inhibitor and represents the culmination of negative and false ideas and concepts that have attached themselves to your belief system. This includes but is not limited to any experiences or events that have caused you fear, pain, rejection, or abandonment. These kinds of experiences and events can produce obstacles, cause struggles, and create troubles in a person's life that hinder them from ever reaching their potential or becoming what they were designed to be. What most people don't realize is that they do have the power to move beyond these hindrances. All humans are born with the power to overcome their obstacles, endure their struggles, and outlast their troubles. They simply need to know how to activate and use that power.

The most powerful inhibitor a person can have is an emotional inhibitor. An emotional inhibitor is a stronghold in a person's life that governs his mind and will. It keeps him from growing beyond the emotional gap that has been created by the hurt or pain associated with the event that onset the emotion. Most people settle on this side of the emotional gap and never even try to bridge the abyss of fear and lies that are now filling the gap. It is this process that facilitates the growth of the underachiever.

It's not where you are emotionally. It's where you choose to stay. **We continue to think the way we think, act the way we act, and feel the way we feel for one reason and one reason alone . . . . our perception of reality and knowledge of truth.**

Most people think that their ability to choose gives them power and control. That is a misconception. The power is not in the choice but in the freedom to choose. Depending on the choice you make, freedom can be taken from you. But when you have truly been made free, your choices are made with a different motivation and the results of your choices do not affect your freedom. This kind of freedom can only be attained through truth. It is truth that sets one free and then he is free indeed.

The only constant in life is truth. Truth reveals purpose, unveils destiny, and causes identity to be discovered. Truth can be clearly seen in all of creation and even in each of us. It is truth that holds our world together.

There are some who use there power to keep others from realizing this truth . . . . that they too are powerful. There are those in this world who attempt to steer others to live there lives by cause and effect. Because someone hurt you, you must hurt others or yourself. Because your parents were one way, you have to be the same way. Because your life has been difficult, you're bound to failure. Because you've made some mistakes, you can no longer dream. The only cause that matters is purpose and the only effect that counts is fulfilling that purpose.

Why dream?

There is indeed something very special about you. You were created to do something unique in your time and space. You were born to be great. Something was placed inside of you and designed to impact your world. It is your dream. Your dream is your pathway to greatness and you can get on the path at any stage of life.

Why is it so important to dream? Your dream is like a window between your past and your future through which you move from where you were to where you were designed to be. It's the vehicle God wants to use to bless your future and make it greater than your past.

Your dream is your ability to turn anything in your life into anything you want it to be. It is your power to get or have your needs, wants, hopes, and desires. It is your license to create something out of nothing. It is your right to explore the unknown. It is the ticket to your tomorrow. It is the key that unlocks your potential. It is your privilege to imagine the possibilities. It is your opportunity to live life the way it was meant to be lived.

If you are to live life the way it was meant to be lived, you *must* dream. If you are to dream, you *must* dethrone the underachiever within you. The greatest human struggle today is the struggle to fight off the underachiever, the image of ourselves that is contrary to our design. This struggle is one of the primary reasons why our young people have such a difficult time with their true identity and self-image. We have moved so far away from the truth that, for some, the truth no longer exists as a valid option, but rather an outdated myth. And so we struggle today with losing our teens and young adults to alternatives to truth that are designed to steer them away from the real truth and keep them distanced from purpose and destiny. Yes, there is an all out attack to keep our young people, in particular, from finding out the truth about who they really are.

Why poetry?

I started a journey several years ago that changed the direction of my life and set me on a collision course with destiny. It was on a fourth Sunday morning in January of 1990 that I was introduced to the question that would consume my life for the next ten years. Answering that question became one of my highest priorities. That day marked the end of my search for significance and the beginning of my reach for greatness. The journey has taken me through the roughest, toughest times of my life. The pursuit of the answer to the question has led me into the unknown, the uncharted, the unfamiliar, and the unexplained. During this time, I've had my highest highs and lowest lows. I've had my greatest times of revelation as well as my greatest times of confusion. I've experienced great power and great weakness, great pride and great humility, great insight and great mystery. I've had the opportunity to become very passionate about what I now see as the new American dream, the pursuit of purpose.

Poetry has been an instrumental vehicle in my pursuit of purpose. It has served as a means of discovery, definition, clarification, communication, and resilience in my life. I have enjoyed poetry for as long as I can remember. Some of my earliest memories of this affinity include listening to a gentleman by the name of Nipsy Russell who once frequented a game show called "The $10,000 Pyramid" in which Dick Clark was the host. Dick would always end the show with words of wisdom from Nipsy whenever he was on. Nipsy would always seem to have the right thing to say at the right time and it would always have the right affect on the listening audience, which included me. He had a knack for putting words together that, not only rhymed and sounded good, but also seemed perfect for the message that he was portraying. This combination of the right words at the right time portraying the right message, compounded by a positive attitude, brilliant smile and magnetic personality could do no less than inspire, encourage, and uplift an impressionable youngster like me.

Well, that show went off the air but my love for poetry continued to grow. I was fascinated with reading and writing poetry and seemed to have my own knack for putting words together. In fact, my speech teacher in High School wrote in my senior yearbook, "TJ, I am really impressed with your writing ability. I hope you will continue to write. Being able to put thoughts on paper is a gift and I am sure you have this gift". It wasn't, however, until my life hit it's lowest point that I really began to express myself through writing. I was able to discover and experience the true nature and power of the written and spoken word. I was able to tap a source of strength deep within me that carried me through this rough period of my life. I learned that I had the ability to frame my future and shape my destiny with the words I said about myself. I discovered the power to remake my life through positive confessions and projections of my past, present, and future. Consequently, I am now living in the future that I framed several years ago with words that I said about myself.

It was during this time that I discovered 'poetry therapy', or poetry used for healing and growth. I had never heard of such a thing even though it could be traced through documentation as far back as the fourth millennium B.C. in ancient Egypt. I learned that it is a discipline in which you can become licensed and registered with the state and that helping professionals all over the world use it to treat their patients. It was at this point that I really began to develop my passion for poetry. I had always gotten a unique sense of accomplishment and fulfillment from selling people on the idea of their own greatness and even projected myself as a motivational speaker. But now it seemed I was standing right in the midst of a defining moment in my life. I had been using my own poetry as a tool to motivate and encourage myself during some really rough times. I had learned how to say to myself what I wanted someone else to say to me. I had learned how to proclaim out of my own mouth what I wanted to be and do through poetic expression. Thus, I had learned how to heal and grow through poetry.

Out of this experience, 'motivational poetry' was birthed. What is motivational poetry? If you want a definition, it is any poetic expression that *insights the mind* with revelation that *encourages the heart* to be stronger and *inspires the will* to do something that *raises the spirit* to another level. If you want to know what the motivational poetry experience is like, then imagine living in a voice-activated world where you could change anything in your life to anything you wanted by simply saying it out of your mouth. Imagine that this power could only be activated by your unique ability to see the change before it happened. Imagine that this unique ability would rely on the accuracy of your thoughts and feelings. Imagine that the accuracy of your thoughts and feelings would depend largely on the degree to which you analyze and scrutinize every word you hear and speak. This, of course, would presuppose that you would have to have the right and ability to accept or reject any words that could potentially lead to ideas, concepts, or beliefs that would produce thoughts and feelings that were unwanted or inaccurate. Do you think that you could make your dreams come true in a world like this? Well, motivational poetry makes this world a reality.

I have now coined this phrase and begun teaching this process to teenagers, young adults, and even older adults. We meet and learn how to interpret out feelings, manage our emotions, think critically, deepen our understanding of self, read and write expressively, frame our futures, and shape our destinies. We utilize motivational poetry, rap, creative writing, storytelling, and rap sessions to facilitate inner healing and personal growth.

A Dreamer's Diary is a compilation of motivational poetry pieces that reflect the true nature and power of the art. I've also written two poetic musicals, *Apples of Gold* and *Rhythmology*, which further demonstrate the awesome ability of the poem to add to the quality of life.

"Believe great things about yourself, say great things to yourself, and you will do great things with yourself!"

The Motivational Poet

The Tour

I want you to listen closely,

Listen very closely to me.

I am about to deliver the words

That are going to set you free.

You'll hear something that will stir you,

Something also that will challenge you,

Maybe something you've never considered,

But it's all to inspire you.

I want you to know for certain

Beyond any shadow of doubt

What this thing you call your life

Is really all about.

So sit back, relax, and

Let your spirit soar

As the Motivational Poet

Takes you on a mental tour.

"You are a unique, one-of-a-kind, never-been-before, never-will-be-again, untapped, undiscovered, unexplored, exotic, priceless, and rare find, treasure, jewel, phenomenal experience and expression of God!"

Don't Let Anyone Tell You Anything Different!

The Motivational Poet

Purpose, The First Order

An idea is born
Into the heart and mind of a man.
The world has not seen it or heard it
Because it does not yet exist.

Time is of the essence.
Belief is vitally crucial.
It must be embraced
If it is to have a future.

The home it has known,
It now wants no more;
For it can no longer survive
In the land of no growth.

The man of the heart and mind
Is he who must be reborn;
For light has come to his world
And darkness must not live on.

Death is the end
That follows his unbelief.
Life is synonymous
With his choice to receive.
The idea has come
From the Great Giver himself,
The Ultimate Dreamer, the One
Who sees all, knows all, and is all.

His purpose is to express
The essence of his being;
The simplicity of his love;
Life's true meaning.

With one little idea
And one simple man,
He, the Greater Giver,
The Ultimate Dreamer, GOD
Is able to reveal his outstretched hand.

Write a statement about yourself, relative to this poem, that you can begin to use to positively shape your thoughts and feelings.

_____

_____

_____

_____

No Matter Where You Are

Ladies and Gentlemen,
  Sisters and Brothers,
    Let me take a moment
      To encourage you to discover

      The dream in your heart,
    The purpose for your life,
  The destiny that awaits you;
The time is here and now.

You can't afford to waste
  Anymore time making a living.
    God is requiring you to embrace
      What he's already given;

      That is life more abundantly
    And all that pertains to it.
  The decision is yours
As to how you're going to use it.

He's given you a pattern
  That you can go by;
    But you must find the rhythm;
      It will speak and not lie.
      You must begin today
    For tomorrow is not promised you.
  Yesterday can no longer help;
Only the right now that is in front of you.

So make your choice now
   And don't wait to decide
      If you are going to face your future
         Or just run and hide.

      If you choose to run and hide,
     You won't get very far
   Because purpose will find you
No matter where you are.

Write a statement about yourself, relative to this poem, that you can begin to use to positively shape your thoughts and feelings.

_____

_____

_____

_____

The Silver Glass

Who is this I see
Looking back at me
When I stand to my feet
And stare into the silver glass intensely?

What is his name?
What is his claim?
Is he proud of his existence
Or is he ashamed?

Does he know who he is
Or which way he's to go?
Does he have any idea
What his life has in store?

Is he aware of his purpose
Or what he has to give?
Does he have that hunger
It takes to truly live?

Is he aggressively
Seeking every opportunity
To make full proof of his life
And his potentiality?

Is this the day he'll say
I can, I will, I must?
Or will he turn down another opportunity
To increase his faith and trust?

The answer to these, my friend,
Lies within the image you see.
As you stare into the silver glass,
Make certain you answer truthfully!

Write a statement about yourself, relative to this poem, that you can begin to use to positively shape your thoughts and feelings.

_____

_____

_____

_____

My Life

What is this life of mine all about?
    What am I suppose to do with it?
    Should I just rely on fate or
Should I aggressively pursue it?

Will I reach my desired end
    With little or no effort of my own?
    Is there something I'm supposed to be doing?
Are there seeds that need to be sown?

What will be the consequences
    If I don't reach my destination?
    What will be the benefits
If I follow all the right directions?

And who is going to show me
    The path that I'm to take?
    Will there be some great barrier
Through which I'm to break?

Is time working against me
    Or do I have as long as I need?
    Do I have a team to support me
Or am I all alone in this world of greed?

Will my questions be answered
    In a swift and timely manner?
    Will there be someone to mentor me
Through the process of getting better?

Can I be assured of victory
    In spite and regardless of everything?
    And will I earn a place in glory
Away from this earthly scene?

These are some questions
    I have about my life;
    The answers I will know
When the time is right.

Write a statement about yourself, relative to this poem, that you can begin to use to positively shape your thoughts and feelings.

_____

_____

_____

_____

To The Heart

Straight to the heart

    Is the best way to go

        Right past the mind

            And what you think you know.

For knowledge is useless

    Without a purpose.

        It fades away,

            Never penetrating the surface.

The center of man

    Is where his life began.

        It's the place where GOD

            First put his hand.

He made each one of us

    From the inside out

        With a special mission

            That tells what we're all about.

So if you want to know

    Just who I am,

        You'll have to look beyond the package

        And into the heart of the man.

Write a statement about yourself, relative to this poem, that you can begin to use to positively shape your thoughts and feelings.

_____

_____

_____

_____

Today, I Find Out

I've had many obstacles in my life

And some situations I've had to face.

I've suffered some wrongdoings

And some bad choices I've made.

It's not my fault,

Although I am responsible.

I did not request to come here,

But I'm here and called to something.

I need to know what that is;

I need to find out soon.

I need to be healed

So that my life can begin to bloom.

I need someone to help me;

Show me how to proceed.

I need someone to watch over me,

Care for me, and help me to protect my seed.

I may not know right now

What this life of mine is about;

But this one thing is for certain,

Today, I will begin to find out.

Write a statement about yourself, relative to this poem, that you can begin to use to positively shape your thoughts and feelings.

_____

_____

_____

_____

The Identity

I am a branch
That grows from the vine.

My mission is to rise
As high as I can,
As long as I can,
Bearing as much fruit as I can
Along the way.

No one can stop me
Because I am connected to the vine.

If you cut me,
I'll grow longer, stronger, and faster.
If you put something in my way,
I'll go over it, around it, sometimes even under it,
Or I'll find a crack and go through it.

I'll embrace every obstacle along the way,
Using each one as a rung on a ladder.

Every adversity gives me
The strength I need to climb.
Every triumph gives me
The courage and hunger I need
To prepare for the next level.

This is my destiny.
This is who I am;
For I was born to rise.

Write a statement about yourself, relative to this poem, that you can begin to use to positively shape your thoughts and feelings.

_____

_____

_____

_____

you Try

You try to take me out
    Every chance you get.
You try to bring me down;
    You want to make me quit.

You set up roadblocks and
    Stumbling blocks in my way.
    You think that will make me forget
What I have to say.

You attempt to make me feel
    Like everything's going wrong.
You wanna make me doubt
    Everything I've got going on.

You try to steal my dream.
    You try to squash my vision.
    You try to quiet my positive vibe.
You wanna thwart my mission.

You try to break my concentration
    And make me focus on the negative.
You try to throw me off my game
    And cause my efforts to be ineffective.

You think your measly suggestions
    Carry some kind of weight with me.
    You fail to realize that I've caught a glimpse
Of what I was designed to be.

You try to make me believe
    That I'm destined for the grave.
But what you don't know is that
    I'm like my brother Dave.

I can hit you with a song.
    I can hit you with a poem.
    I can hit you with a dance.
You never know how I'm flowin'.

I can come up out of your mess
    With all kinds of revelation,
Springing forth and bursting out,
    Driving me towards my destination.

I can take your cheap shot
    And swallow your bitter pill.
    I can handle your slander
And dismantle your dirty deal.

Your tricks don't hold a candle
    To my truth and triumph.
Your deception is no match
    For my determination and desire.

I can take everything you throw at me
    And use it to my advantage.
    You can't begin to compete with me because
I was created to have dominion!

Write a statement about yourself, relative to this poem, that you can begin to use to positively shape your thoughts and feelings.

_____
_____
_____
_____

Attitude

I came into this world
In a very peculiar way.

I did not ask to come,
But I am here to stay.

I'll stay until I'm done
With what I came to do.

I'll be here until I'm sure
That all my work is through.

And when I'm done I'll leave
With nothing in my hand.

For my attitude is to give
As long and as much as I can.

This may just seem like
A simple way to live.

But it seems that life is multiplied
To those who are willing to give!

Write a statement about yourself, relative to this poem, that you can begin to use to positively shape your thoughts and feelings.

_____

_____

_____

_____

The Response

They came to get me
 And I wasn't at home.

They called for me
 And I wasn't receiving calls.

They yelled out my name
 And I did not answer.

They wrote me a letter
 And I didn't write back;
  I didn't even read it.

They prayed for me.

 They yearned for me.

They moaned over me.

 They cried for me.

They sacrificed for me.

They gave all they could give.
They did all they could do.

They said all they could say.

And finally, one day,
Out of the blue,

From deep within me

Came the response;

And the response was

Yes Lord!

Write a statement about yourself, relative to this poem, that you can begin to use to positively shape your thoughts and feelings.

_____

_____

_____

_____

True Passion

True passion is like a fire
That burns from deep within.

You try to put it out or disregard it,
Only to have it surface more powerful again.

The need is to become a student
And find the origin of this great desire,

The purpose of it's ever burning flame,
The destiny it longs to claim.

From where come
The longings of the heart?

Come they from things
Seen or heard or thought,

Things inherited, absorbed,
Attracted, or caught?

One must look within, deep within
To find the answer!

A look into the soul
Reveals these matters more.

Write a statement about yourself, relative to this poem, that you can begin to use to positively shape your thoughts and feelings.

_____

_____

_____

_____

For The Record

In case you didn't know
Because no one told you so,
I am supposed to be here.

I thought I couldn't take it.
They said I wouldn't make it;
But here I am despite my every fear.

Yes, it was rough
And sometimes even tough;
But through it all I came.

The words of my testimony
Are surely not the only
Reason that I'm winning this game.

So let me fill you in
On the Master and His plan
To make certain that victory was mine.

He paid a price for me
One day on Calvary
That was good for all people and all times.

Write a statement about yourself, relative to this poem, that you can begin to use to positively shape your thoughts and feelings.

_____

_____

_____

_____

The Dream

Say you've got a dream
        Ringing in your heart?
        Well, get ready my friend,
        Your pain is about to start!

Set yourself now
        For all kinds of opposition.
        Prepare to regroup daily;
        This is going to be a tough mission.

Fortify your mind.
        Anticipate all negative.
        Keep your mouth loaded
        With positive affirmation.

Set a guard at your heart
        To keep the thieves away.
        They're out to steal your dream
        And replace it with dismay.

Be well acquainted with
        Your motives and intent.
        You'll need to be sure-footed,
        Steadfast, and persistent.

Hear the voice of wisdom;
> Bind her around you neck.
> Let the spirit of the dream-giver
> Always keep you in check.

Rehearse your reason why;
> It is necessary everyday.
> Make no provision for
> Your enemy to come in and stay.

Press on towards the mark,
> The goal you set so high.
> The dream that seemed so far away
> Is now near and close by.

So don't even think about
> Giving up my friend.
> The manifestation of your dream
> Is just around the bend!

Write a statement about yourself, relative to this poem, that you can begin to use to positively shape your thoughts and feelings.

_____

_____

_____

_____

Never The Same

It seemed my life

    Was going nowhere

        Trapped without hope

           In endless despair

No one available
    For me to confide in
        Abused, misused, confused
           Wanted my life to end

Self-destructive behavior

    Became my medicine

        Too much, too soon, too late

           The cycle already reeled me in

Beaten down so far
    I thought I'd lose my mind
        Until the Savior of the world
           Rescued me right on time

He told me about my future

    The plans He prepared for me

        He told me about His love

            How He sent His son to die for me

Now I call him Lord
    Yea, Jesus is his name
        Because of what He's done
            My life will never be the same.

Write a statement about yourself, relative to this poem, that you can begin to use to positively shape your thoughts and feelings.

_____

_____

_____

_____

R
e
a
c
h
D
e
e
p

Reach deep, reach deep I say
Into you heart of hearts.

Find the thing that you want most
And from you, never let it part.

Work each day diligently,
If you want it to come to past.

Little by little, bit by bit
Builds a foundation that will last.

Consistently speak words of wisdom,
Words of encouragement too.

You'll need every positive thing
To help you press on through.

The destiny is what you want,
The end that reveals the glory.

You'll find within, as it unfolds,
The revelation of your life's story!

Write a statement about yourself, relative to this poem, that you can begin to use to positively shape your thoughts and feelings.

_____

_____

_____

_____

The Mind's eye What one thinks he is . . . . he is

What one thinks he will be . . . . he will be

Where one thinks he is at . . . . he is there

Where one thinks he is going . . . . he will arrive

How one sees his world . . . . that's how it is

How one views his life . . . . that's how it plays out

What one says . . . . he cannot escape

What one feels . . . . he cannot deny

What one does . . . . he cannot reverse

The word of one's mouth

The expression of one's heart

The work of one's hand

Paint a picture of the mind's eye.

Write a statement about yourself, relative to this poem, that you can begin to use to positively shape your thoughts and feelings.

_____

_____

_____

_____

Raising The Bar

What do you expect
    Out of your life today?
        Will your dream be furthered
            Or will it be delayed?
Will you reach high
    To your fullest extent
        For what you say will
            Make your heart content?
Will today be full
    Of opportunistic preparation
        Guiding you towards
            Your dream's manifestation?
Will you only make
    Confessions of faith
        That set your mind
            And guard your way?
Don't you know
    You'll most likely get
        Whatever it is
        That you expect?
You must endeavor
    To look and see
        That you life is not
        One of mediocrity.
You must "raise the bar"
    And take it to another level.
        This is not the time for doubting,
            Nor the hour to be fearful.

You must learn to expect
    More from yourself
        And not be afraid to
            Reach for that top shelf.
You may just find that
    Things are not as difficult
        When you study to apply
            The right patterns and principles.

So go ahead, prepare yourself,
    And reach for your star!
        You can only do this
            By "raising the bar"!

Write a statement about yourself, relative to this poem, that you can begin to use to positively shape your thoughts and feelings.

_____

_____

_____

_____

Change

Change is an event
      That needs no one's permission.

      One way or the other
It happens of its own volition.

The time to adjust
      Is before the change comes,

      Prior to the need,
While today's work is still undone.

Change is a necessity
      For development and growth.

      It is your ability to advance,
Your opportunity to go forth.

Frustration is the precursor,
      The sign plate on the door.

      It lets us know the time
Before the clock will show.

Resisting change is futile;
      You cannot because it already is.

      Follow the natural order of things
To the place where destiny lives.

Write a statement about yourself, relative to this poem, that you can begin to use to positively shape your thoughts and feelings.

_____

_____

_____

_____

The Mind-Shift

Hear these words;
Embrace them I say.
The time has come
For a mind-shift to take place.

Be no longer bound
By ignorance of past.
God has equipped you
To accomplish a task.

See your value.
Know your worth.
Express your ability
To be His image in the earth.

Appreciate your uniqueness.
Let man define your not.
Look inside of yourself
And recognize what you've got.

Receive no pressure
From anyone to conform.
Renew your mind daily
That you may be transformed.

Walk in the passion
And burden of your dream,
Meaning what you say
And saying what you mean.

Take heed to the restraints
And liberties of your heart;
Without them it is impossible
To complete what you start.

And finally, rise up,
Go and take your land;
Disciplining all nations
And teaching all men!

Write a statement about yourself, relative to this poem, that you can begin to use to positively shape your thoughts and feelings.

_____
_____
_____
_____

Obedience Is

Obedience is a decision and not an act

  It is a result of faith and not fate

    It is born out of love and not duty

      It brings forth blessings and not curses

    It produces pleasure and not frustration

  It is freedom and not bondage

It is a choice that only you can make.

Write a statement about yourself, relative to this poem, that you can begin to use to positively shape your thoughts and feelings.

_____

_____

_____

_____

The Lesson

No one really knows
Who you are
       Until you rise and
       Show them you're a star.

Not the kind that
Gets all of the attention,
       But the kind that
       Shines bright and glistens.

No one really knows
Where you've been
       Until you open you mouth
       And testify again;

Telling your story
From cover to cover;
       Sharing your experience
       Like no other.

No one knows what
You've gone through;
       They only see what
       You have come to.

For it doesn't matter
Which way you've gone,
      The things you got right or
      The things you got wrong.

What matters is what you've learned
And who you've become
      Since the day you left
      The place you came from.

You see if you are in touch
With who you are now,
      Then no one can ever stop you,
      No way, no how!

Write a statement about yourself, relative to this poem, that you can begin to use to positively shape your thoughts and feelings.

_____
_____
_____
_____

Doors of Life

The doors of life bring many questions
That must be answered quickly

Make the right decision
Or opportunity will fade swiftly

Time is rarely a friend
So be diligent to examine

The path that leads to many doors
May also lead to famine

Evaluate the circumstance
Analyze the condition

Make the change necessary
Maintain growth permission

Don't crave the least resistant
But cleave to persistence

Make an open shame
Of everything that defies your name.

Write a statement about yourself, relative to this poem, that you can begin to use to positively shape your thoughts and feelings.

_____

_____

_____

_____

The Winner

This race is not given

      To the swift nor strong,

But to the one who continues on.

This contest is not won

      By the one with the most points,

But by the one steadfast in little triumphs.

This prize is not awarded

      To the one with the highest score

But to the one willing to endure.

This game is played

      By winners only;

Those who play skillfully,

      Passionately, and humbly.

      The game is life!
      The race is to eternity!

      The contest is fulfillment of purpose!
      The prize is happiness!

Who is the winner?

He who achieves happiness

      Through the fulfillment of his purpose

            As he lives out eternity!

Write a statement about yourself, relative to this poem, that you can begin to use to positively shape your thoughts and feelings.

_____

_____

_____

_____

Destined To Win

I am the head
And not the tail
I am above only
And not beneath

I am blessed in the city
And in the field
I am blessed going out
And coming in

I am the lender
And not the borrower
I am the rich
And not the poor

I am more than a conqueror
I am always triumphant
I am highly favored
Among all men

I am like a tree
Planted by a river
Who brings forth fruit and
Whose leaves cannot wither

My delight is in the Lord
    And His law is my meditation
        He's brought me through storms
            Hard times and many frustrations

        I know I will succeed
      It's all part of God's plan
    His word will not fail me
I am destined to win.

Write a statement about yourself, relative to this poem, that you can begin to use to positively shape your thoughts and feelings.

_____

_____

_____

_____

The Press

When your dream gets clouded
With apparent reality,

There is something
You must remember to see.

The picture that's before you
Is definitely not real.

It's only a smoke screen
To keep you standing still.

What you must do
Is make up in your mind

That no weapon formed against
You will make you step aside!

You must say to yourself,
I'm on a straight and narrow path.

I'll help many along the way,
But I will not be side-tracked.

You must press forward
Through your journey, towards the end.

At the point of no return, you must
Reach back for someone who has yet to begin.

With increasing determination
To not be denied,

You must run with character and grace,
Assured of who's on your side.

And when you have reached your goal
And have observed what you've become,

It is then that you will realize
Your dream has only just begun!

Write a statement about yourself, relative to this poem, that you can begin to use to positively shape your thoughts and feelings.

_____
_____
_____
_____

Most Prized Creation

Look at me! Just look at me!
I am beautiful as you can see.
I am wonderfully made and uniquely fashioned
For my creator's presence, just to make Him happy.

He made me with a purpose.
He filled me with a passion.
He validated me with a promise.
He gave me abilities that exceed me.

I can run through troops; I can leap over walls.
I can speak to mountains; I can fly with eagles.
I am His most prized creation.

You may not like what you see,
But I'm sure it's because you don't understand fully.
You see, the one who made me is a master craftsman
And He's able to always get in the end
Exactly what He imagined in the beginning.

He can take what looks like trash
And turn it into a treasure that no man can measure.
He can take the unseemly and unstately
And turn them both into masterpieces of rare beauty.
He can take a ditch filled with muck and mire
And turn it into a pure, refreshing, life-yielding river.

Yes, He can do anything
Because He's already done everything.
And the most awesome part is this
My creator is your creator too
And what He's done in me,
He's also done in you!
We are His most prized creations!

Write a statement about yourself, relative to this poem, that you can begin to use to positively shape your thoughts and feelings.

_____

_____

_____

_____

The Right Stuff

Just because it didn't happen
The first time around,
  The second, the third
    Or the fourth time down

  Doesn't give you the right
To throw in the towel and quit,
  Give up on your dream,
    Or say it doesn't fit.

    You've got to be supercharged
  With belief in yourself,
Knowing that one day soon
  Persistence will wear down resistance and
    Your dream will be in full bloom.

  You've got to stay the course
And not be shaken.
  Hold out and hold on
    To your dream in the making.

  Remember your reason why
And keep your fire burning.
  Ward off the dream-killers
    As you keep your creative juices churning.

Look forward to the day
When your efforts shall reward you.
Be willing to go through
·Whatever you need to.

Know that you are resilient
And never ever give up.
Make your dream a reality.
You can do it 'cause
You've got the right stuff!

Write a statement about yourself, relative to this poem, that you can begin to use to positively shape your thoughts and feelings.

_____
_____
_____
_____

Special one, precious one
Only one like you
Time to let the world see
Your life from God's view
Time to put the past behind
Let old things fade away
Time to let the world hear
What the real you have to say
Time to put into action
All the things you've learned
Time to follow through
Get the blessings and returns
Time to put to test
All the promises of God
Time to finally get
What you've worked for so long and hard
So don't waste anymore time
Go forth into your destiny
Live, learn, love and grow
Into what God created you to be.

Time

73

Write a statement about yourself, relative to this poem, that you can begin to use to positively shape your thoughts and feelings.

_____

_____

_____

_____

Life Is What You Make It

Sometimes life is totally unfair it seems

And those around you don't understand your reasoning.

They feel that you should just let go of your dream

And follow the path of least resistance.

They don't understand that your dream

Is who you are and who you are going to be

And if you let that go you'll be

No good to anyone or for anything.

Life will give up what belongs to you

After you have struggled and fought through.

You have to know who you are and what is yours

Life will open up the world through your dreams doors

You have to foster relentless pursuit

Of the dream you've held inside from your youth

You must never say never and never quit

Because life is not fair, but it is what you make it.

Write a statement about yourself, relative to this poem, that you can begin to use to positively shape your thoughts and feelings.

_____

_____

_____

_____

Continue On

Continue on . . . .

> in the things you've heard.

Continue on . . . .

> your foundation in the word.

Continue on . . . .

> through all opposition.

Continue on . . . .

> until you accomplish you mission.

Continue on . . . .

> regardless and in spite of.

Continue on . . . .

> in your demonstration of love.

Continue on . . . .

> though the waters are rough.

Continue on . . . .

> until God shows up.

Continue on . . . .

> until you pass the end.

Continue on . . . .

> until you win!

Write a statement about yourself, relative to this poem, that you can begin to use to positively shape your thoughts and feelings.

_____

_____

_____

_____

The Craftsman

I love who I am

    And who I was made to be

    Because I was wonderfully made,

        Curious and full of beauty.

I was crafted at the hands of an expert

    Who carefully considered every detail

    As he masterfully laid out his plan

        To bring my life to full scale!

I am his handiwork

    And all his work is good.

    My life has been choreographed

        That I might do what I should.

So when you see me with my head up

    Walking like I know whose I am,

    It's because of Him who made me.

        He is a master craftsman!

Write a statement about yourself, relative to this poem, that you can begin to use to positively shape your thoughts and feelings.

_____

_____

_____

_____

Perseverence

Don't you dare

Throw away your confidence;

For it is a reward

Of great recompense.

Don't be afraid

To experience pain;

For it holds the passion

That will keep you in the game.

Always let patience

Be fully expressed

So that you may endure

The entire process.

Endure with faith

Having great substance.

Accomplish God's will

And you'll receive every promise!

Write a statement about yourself, relative to this poem, that you can begin to use to positively shape your thoughts and feelings.

_____

_____

_____

_____

Flow With Me

When you fight with me,
You fight with all that makes you strong.

When you strive with me,
You strive with all that brings you peace.

When you contend with me,
You contend with all that loves you.

When you war with me,
You war with all that makes you safe.

When you alienate me,
You alienate your future.

But when you flow with me,
You flow with everything
That makes you beautiful and complete.

So come on and flow with me.
My burden is light and my yoke is easy
And I am with you
Every step of the way.

Write a statement about yourself, relative to this poem, that you can begin to use to positively shape your thoughts and feelings.

_____

_____

_____

_____

Meditations

Our thoughts are the most
Intimate thing we possess.
They are, indeed, the deciding
Factor in our success.

They reveal the meditations of our heart.
They show us where change needs to start.

They unveil the feelings
And emotions from our past.
They reveal the shadow of hope
That our future casts.

They remind us of where we have been.
They encourage us to press on towards the end.

The wrong thoughts will destroy expectation.
The right thoughts will fuel determination.

To reach your goal and accomplish your task,
Don't let a day go by that you fail to ask:

Are my thoughts conducive
To where I want to go?
Do they truly reflect who I am
Or what I stand for?

Are they leading me to who I desire to become
Or pushing me back to where I came from?

Think about it and come to an honest conclusion.
Dispel every false image and illusion.
Then renew your thoughts and be free
To meditate on exactly who you are and desire to be!

Write a statement about yourself, relative to this poem, that you can begin to use to positively shape your thoughts and feelings.

_____

_____

_____

_____

The Final Call

What you call trouble,
   I call potential.
      What you call stubbornness,
         I call persistence.

What you call sickness,
   I call healing in action.
      What you call difficult,
         I call proof.

What you call too late,
   I call right on time.
      What you call too high,
         I call within reach.

What you call defeat,
   I call victory.
      What you call failure,
         I call success.

What you call impossible,
   I call probable.
      What you call done, through with, and over,
         I call just getting started.

What you say will never happen,
   I say it's already done.
      What you say will never arrive,
         I say it's already come.

What you call frustration,
    I call the need for change.
        What you call overdue,
            I call special delivery.

What you call confusion,
    I call structure.
        What you call chaos,
            I call order.

What you call trials,
    I call patience.
        What you call hopeless,
            I call hopeful.

What you call time,
    I call opportunity.
        What you call life,
            I call purpose.

Your call is temporary.
    My call is eternal.
        It is your choice only that separates
            Your call from my will.

Who am I?
    I am, of course,
        The One who makes
            The final call.

Write a statement about yourself, relative to this poem, that you can begin to use to positively shape your thoughts and feelings.

_____

_____

_____

_____

Be True To Yourself

When things are failing all around,
    Who will be there holding their ground?
        Be true to yourself!

When the choices you make don't go right,
    Who will continue on beyond sight?
        Be true to yourself!

When life doesn't want to give up your dream,
    Who makes you feel you can do anything?
        Be true to yourself!

When going on is the last thing you want to do,
    Who reminds you that you must go on through?
        Be true to yourself!

You're the one with the dream!

    You're the one willing to do anything!

    You're the one who will go the last mile!

You're the one ready to stand every test and trial!

    So lift up your head and do what you must do!

    For it is to yourself that you must be true!

Write a statement about yourself, relative to this poem, that you can begin to use to positively shape your thoughts and feelings.

_____
_____
_____
_____

The Contract

There was a contract out on my life,
    A design to get rid of me.
    The enemy of my soul
Desired to sift me out like wheat.

He sought to change the course of destiny
    By having me abort my purpose.
    He planned to drain me of my substance
And deplete my life's surplus.

He intended to rob me of my inheritance
    And dislocate me from my legacy.
    He thought he could strip me of my existence
And disconnect me from my family.

As soon as I found out about this contract,
    I immediately and strategically began
    To de-commission the lies and accusations
That were cleverly written therein.

I began to structure my own contract
    Based on the promises of the true and living God;
    The One who made me and planned for me
According to His covenant of love.

I decided to come into agreement
    With the good things already prepared for me.
    I chose to take a stand
Against all manner of negativity.

I started to proclaim and declare some things
    To come to past in my life.
    I began to operate in confidence
Walking by faith and not by sight.

I realized the awesome power
    That had been placed at my disposal.
    I stepped into the greatness
That revealed all that was possible.

And now I walk in that greatness
    Each day I'm allowed to live.
    My creative imagination leads me
Into everything I was destined to have.

Write a statement about yourself, relative to this poem, that you can begin to use to positively shape your thoughts and feelings.

_____
_____
_____
_____

Stand

Though your life seems
Unfair and unyielding,
Know that you can lift up your head,
Gather yourself, and stand!

Though the road you travel
Seems long and hard,
Know that you can lift up your head,
Gather yourself, and stand!

Though your dream seems
Impossible and unattainable,
Know that you can lift up your head,
Gather yourself, and stand!

You see standing is not passive;
It is very much active!

It involves going forward
When it seems you're going backwards!

It means pushing harder
and lasting longer,

Reaching higher
And being stronger!

And when you've done all these things
And still have not realized your dream,
Know that you can lift up your head,

Gather yourself, and stand!

Write a statement about yourself, relative to this poem, that you can begin to use to positively shape your thoughts and feelings.

_____

_____

_____

_____

Here I Am, Here I Come

People want to judge
When they don't understand.
They see my confidence
And call it arrogance.

Don't hate me because I walk
In the power of who I am.
I've been pressed down long enough
And I won't be again.

My time to shine is now
Even though it's not about me.
It's about the one who created me for
And is calling me to my destiny.

There are places I must go.
There are people I must see.
There are lives I must impact.
No time to waste precious commodity.

I'm not in a hurry,
But I am on a mission.
I'm not after glory,
I'm in pursuit of my vision.

This world has never seen
The likes of my uniqueness.
I'm the carrier of a dream
That houses my completeness.

Some say I can't do it,
Others say I won't make it.
But in the end they will all
Recognize the authentic.

So get ready world,
Here I am and here I come.
I didn't ask for your permission
And I don't need your validation.

I'm coming in the power
Of the one who sent me;
The creator of the worlds
From infinity to infinity.

Write a statement about yourself, relative to this poem, that you can begin to use to positively shape your thoughts and feelings.

_____

_____

_____

_____

The Quitting Kind

I'm not the quitting kind.
I have never been.

I was predestined to succeed.
I am supposed to win!

I've had many obstacles
To threaten what I believe.

But each one seemed a confirmation
To the dream that I received.

I'm not the quitting kind.
There's no way I can be.

I've invested too much.
Too much has been invested in me.

If I don't follow my dream
Through to the end,

I'll just frustrate myself
Again and again and again.

I'm not the quitting kind.
No, I say! I'm not!

I am a dreamer!
And to that end,
I will never stop!

Write a statement about yourself, relative to this poem, that you can begin to use to positively shape your thoughts and feelings.

_____

_____

_____

_____

They Were Wrong

They said I couldn't take it.
> They thought I wouldn't make it.
> > They believed I wasn't strong.
> > > But as you can see, they were wrong.

> > > They said I didn't have what it takes.
> > They thought I would crumble and break.
They believed I wouldn't move on.
But as you can see, they were wrong.

They said 'no one cares who you are'.
> They thought 'your life is just too hard'.
> > They believed I wouldn't make it this far.
> > > But as you can see, they were wrong.

> > > They said I wasn't powerful.
> > They thought I was pitiful.
> They believed I could never be useful.
But as you can see, they were wrong.

They didn't understand my dream.
> They didn't know my purpose.
> > They didn't see my true destiny.
> > > And now you can clearly see they were wrong.

Write a statement about yourself, relative to this poem, that you can begin to use to positively shape your thoughts and feelings.

_____
_____
_____
_____

For Hope

Push on in the face of fear.

Press on in the grips of pain.

Tell you mind to hold on!

Urge your heart to be strong!

For hope will never make you ashamed!

Write a statement about yourself, relative to this poem, that you can begin to use to positively shape your thoughts and feelings.

No Matter What It Takes

I'm gonna be a man and take a stand.
  I'm gonna always do the best I can.
I'm gonna make it to my promised land,
  No matter what it takes.

I'm gonna see the positive in everything.
  I'm gonna keep my actions and my attitude clean.
I'm gonna make it to my promised land,
  No matter what it takes.

I'm gonna be sensitive to the needs of others.
  I'm gonna help my sisters and my brothers.
I'm gonna make it to my promised land,
  No matter what it takes.

I'm gonna motivate and encourage those around me.
  I'm gonna share my testimony with humility.
I'm gonna make it to my promised land,
  No matter what it takes.

I'm gonna grow in wisdom and understanding.
  I'm gonna make sure I speak positive things.
I'm gonna make it to my promised land,
  No matter what it takes.

I'm gonna be resilient and persistent.
  I'm gonna be remorseful and repentant.
I'm gonna make it to my promised land,
  No matter what it takes.

I'm gonna laugh, I'm gonna cry
    And I won't be afraid to die.
I'm gonna make it to my promised land,
    No matter what it takes

When I come to the end of my road
    And it's all said and done,
The race I will have run
    Will end in my promised land.

Write a statement about yourself, relative to this poem, that you can begin to use to positively shape your thoughts and feelings.

_____

_____

_____

_____

I Can, I Will, I Must

I can be the best
                At anything I do.

I will do my best
                In all of the things I choose.

I must give my best
                In everything I go through.

I can accomplish any task
                To which I set my mind.

I will reach every goal
                That I set in due time.

I must finish everything I start
                Leaving nothing undone behind.

I can love others
                The way I want to be loved.

I will prefer others
                Regardless and in spite of.

I must serve others
                With the heart and spirit that's from above.

Write a statement about yourself, relative to this poem, that you can begin to use to positively shape your thoughts and feelings.

_____

_____

_____

_____

Take My Shame, But Not My Pain

I was down and out
And couldn't pay my bills.
I had no job,
Just valleys with no hills.
> Lord take my shame, but not my pain!

My business had failed.
My reputation was frail.
My credibility had been nailed
> Lord take my shame, but not my pain!

My wife was angry with me,
My kids were disappointed in me,
And You, I couldn't hear nor see.
> Lord take my shame, but not my pain!

My peers were counting me out.
My friends seemed in doubt.
All I could do was scream and shout.
> Lord take my shame, but not my pain!

I wanted to break free,
But my failures held me in captivity.
Was this how it was meant to be?
> Lord take my shame, but not my pain!

Then I asked the Lord to help me
To hold on to my victory
Even though I was facing misery.
    And he took my shame, but not my pain!

Now when I think of my pain,
  I think of my power.
    When I think of my trials,
      I think of my triumph.

Lord thank you for taking my shame, but not my pain!

Write a statement about yourself, relative to this poem, that you can begin to use to positively shape your thoughts and feelings.

_____

_____

_____

_____

Easy Living

Increase the peace,
Reduce the stress.
Don't let a little fox
Become a big mess.

Think on the positive,
Eliminate the negative.
Why should you make
Your troubles indefinite?

Life is full of twists and turns.
In fact it is a cycle you need to discern.

There are times of prosperity;
Be thankful and enjoy.
There are times of adversity;
Adjust, go on, there's more!

Life is not about things
Always going your way.
It's about the chance to give
That lies within each day.

So look to the hills, my friend;
For life is bigger than you.
But know beyond any doubt
That life also includes you!

Write a statement about yourself, relative to this poem, that you can begin to use to positively shape your thoughts and feelings.

_____

_____

_____

_____

Or What

Make it or fake it!

Endure or fade away!

Believe the truth or reject it!

Be healed or remain diseased!

Overcome or succumb!

Become great or grow obsolete!

Walk in victory or wallow in defeat!

Stand up and be counted or sit idle and be overlooked!

Tell the world who you are or remain a stranger to yourself!

Have the joy you want or keep the sadness you have!

Love and be loved without condition or fear without hope!

Make life happen or wonder what could have happened!

Write a statement about yourself, relative to this poem, that you can begin to use to positively shape your thoughts and feelings.

_____

_____

_____

_____

No Pain, No Gain

If you're not willing to be sick,
> Then you're not ready for health.

If you're not willing to be poor,
> Then you're not ready for wealth.

If you're not willing to be weak,
> Then you're not ready for strength.

If you're not willing to be frustrated,
> Then you're not ready for contentment.

If you're not willing to be rejected,
> Then you're not ready for success.

If you're not willing to have your hope deferred,
> Then you're not ready to be blessed.

Write a statement about yourself, relative to this poem, that you can begin to use to positively shape your thoughts and feelings.

_____

_____

_____

_____

The Defining Moment

There comes a moment in life
    When time just stands still;
The moment of passion,
    The moment of purpose,
The moment a man discovers
    What makes him who he is.

Oh, in that moment
    There seems to be no end
To the fire burning within him
    That lights the path to where he's destined.

Power surges within him.
    His dreams are as clear as day.
The events of his life flash before him.
    He sees them now in a whole new way.

He gains a new understanding
    Of all his hurt and pain.
He feels the strength and fortitude
    That has arisen from his disdain.

He looks back over his relationships,
    Especially those gone sour.
He discerns how each one
    Has prepared him for this hour.

He sees himself standing boldly and
    Yet anxiously on the brink of change.
He recognizes that his life
    Will never again be the same.

This moment produces a resilience
    Like he's never known before.
He beams with a radiance
    That emanates from his very core.

Yes, this is the defining moment;
    The one that reveals the script,
The script that tells the story,
    The story of your life's intent.

Strange, it may seem.
    Funny, it may even feel.
Weird, it may appear to be.
    But right, you know it is.

Face it! You cannot deny it.
    Embrace it! You cannot fight it.
Pursue it! You cannot reverse it.
    Become it! You cannot undo it.

Write a statement about yourself, relative to this poem, that you can begin to use to positively shape your thoughts and feelings.

_____

_____

_____

_____

When it's time to risk it all,
Move beyond your fear.
When it's time to make the tough call,
Move beyond your fear.

When it's time to work your plan,
Move beyond your fear.
When it's time to take a stand,
Move beyond your fear.

When it's time to make a change,
Move beyond your fear.
When it's time to rearrange,
Move beyond your fear.

Fear is the surest way
To imprison creativity;
The pathway to advancement,
The doorway to opportunity.

Don't let fear trap you
And cause you to miss your timing;
Your opportunity for promotion,
Your chance to keep on climbing.

To miss your timing is to miss
A conditionally favorable opportunity
To accomplish a certain task or thing
In a given moment of creativity.

You must take action now,
While the given moment is here.
The quickest way to action
Is to move beyond your fear!

Write a statement about yourself, relative to this poem, that you can begin to use to positively shape your thoughts and feelings.

_____
_____
_____
_____

I'm determined
> To be free
> To be happy
> To be me

I'm determined
> To make it
> To take it
> And not to fake it

I'm determined
> To be thankful
> To be hopeful
> To be faithful

I'm determined
> To press on
> To push on
> To keep on
> And to move on

I'm determined
> To be mindful
> To be careful
> To be prayerful

I'm determined
> To be optimistic
> To be realistic
> To be altruistic

I'm determined
> To live my dreams
> Fulfill my purpose
> And reach my destiny.

Write a statement about yourself, relative to this poem, that you can begin to use to positively shape your thoughts and feelings.

_____

_____

_____

_____

Strange Place

When you find yourself in a certain place
And you don't know how you got there;
You don't like that you are there; and
You don't know how you're going
To get away from there,

Realize and know that fear
Is standing at the door,
Waiting to come in
To distort your view of the end,
And ultimately discredit
The ability you have within.

So what do you do?
You press on through
And make your insecurities
Fewer than few.
You deal with fear
By going the distance,
Eliminating doubt in that very instance.

Beyond where you are
Is everything you're looking for.
But you must find truth
If you are going to produce
In the place you're in
As well as the place you're going.
And hey, let's face it!

Being productive is what it's all about.
A life of anything less
Is certainly a life without
Joy, peace, happiness, love.
You know, the things we all dream of.

So maybe this place is not so strange after all.
Maybe it's just an opportunity to stand tall
And be the person you were meant to be.
For this is your heritage, right, and destiny!

Therefore seize the moment
While in the strange place.
For it is your life
Staring you in the face.
Be bold about it and have no fear!
Turn the experience into a life-changing affair.

Write a statement about yourself, relative to this poem, that you can begin to use to positively shape your thoughts and feelings.

_____

_____

_____

_____

I Am Purpose

I was an *idea*
   Created in the mind of God.

I soon became a *word*
   Spoken out of His mouth.

Not long after I became a *seed*
   Implanted in my Daddy's loins.

I went on to become a *living, breathing creature*
   Sown into my Mother's womb.

It was just a matter of time before I became a *functioning organism*
   Delivered into the world.

And now I am . . . . An idea in reality

         A word in action

         A seed in growth

         A creation in process

         An organism at work

         A purpose being fulfilled

Write a statement about yourself, relative to this poem, that you can begin to use to positively shape your thoughts and feelings.

_____

_____

_____

_____

The Passion of Purpose

For the joy that is set before me,
I press towards this that I see.

When I close my eyes and open them again,
There still is this thing waiting to come in.

It wants to become the driving force in my life,
Steered by the creators' sovereign plan.

Though I've never completely given myself to
This thing, I feel as if I am already one with it.

I've even seen a glimpse of the finished product,
The destination, and deep within me, there is an
Abiding sense of victory.

I'm sure I cannot lose because I somehow know
That I was born to do this.

So now here I stand
With but one question to answer still.

Do I or do I not embrace this path
And fulfill His will.

I must conclude without reason or excuse.
There is absolutely, positively
Nothing else for me to do.

Write a statement about yourself, relative to this poem, that you can begin to use to positively shape your thoughts and feelings.

_____

_____

_____

_____

The Sovereign Hour

I see your hurt.
   I feel your pain.
I hear your heart.
   I know your shame.

You've been deceived.
   You've been let down.
      You've been misinformed.
         Now it's time to turn it around.

This is the sovereign hour
   In which you must find out the truth
About the purpose and destiny
   That has been assigned to you.

It's time to take fear and kick it to the curb.
   It's time to take doubt and replace it with the Word.

It's time to recognize the power you have within,
   Your creative ability to accomplish anything.

It's time to realize the status of the game.
   You've been declared the winner
      On the authority in His name.

You have the legal right
   To begin taking back
All that was taken from you,
   Everything you were denied in lack.

You've been given the power of a tongue,
   The authority to frame your future,
      The ability to set your destiny,
         The right to have dominion over all the earth.

You are now standing on the brink of your greatest desire.
   Get ready to embark upon your finest hour.

This is how it's going down;
   So get with the program.
The Will of the Sovereign Creator
   Is about to take you to another realm.

Write a statement about yourself, relative to this poem, that you can begin to use to positively shape your thoughts and feelings.

_____

_____

_____

_____

The No Limits Way

Learn with an open mind,
Considering the possibilities;
For life reaches far beyond
    Your personal limits and boundaries.

Love with a pure heart,
Free from conditions that bind.
Utilize your feelings and emotions
    As you follow your life's outline.

Laugh with full expression,
Recognizing the humor in life;
For earthly things are full of vanity
    And man's purpose is the end of his plight.

Live as if there's no tomorrow;
For who's to say tomorrow will be.
Remember yesterday and respect today.
    Find your passion amidst your reality.

Leave a legacy for those
Who remain after you are long gone.
Promote the patterns and principles
    That will cause your legacy to live on.

And finally, let your life
Speak in conclusion and say . . . .
This one knew how to live;
    For he lived, she lived the 'no limits' way!

Write a statement about yourself, relative to this poem, that you can begin to use to positively shape your thoughts and feelings.

_____

_____

_____

_____

How I Got Over

Resilience is the key!
 Resilience is the key;
Even though it might appear
 That your fate will not end in victory.

Look with a different eye,
 One that sees beyond the surface.
An eye unlike that of the spy
 Who sees those things that are worthless.

Passion is the fuel!
 Passion is the fuel!
Add it to vision to create a formula
 That can't be stopped by limitations or rules.

Follow your heart
 And be led by what is deepest inside.
You'll discover that every obstacle
 Is a direct result of divine design.

Retire your doubt on the determination
 That things are not as they seem.
Have in hand the gripping truth
 About who you were born to be.

Rest on the testimonies
 Of those who have gone before you.
Cling to the promises
 Attached to "that thing" you've been called to.

Throw fear a farewell party,
　　Complete with cake, ice cream, and hats.
Mean it in your heart and fix it in your mind
　　That fear won't be coming back.

When failure and frustration try to reacquaint with you,
　　Tell them you've moved on.
The days of back and forth and up and down
　　Have long since been gone.

When rejection and abandonment take a trip to your house,
　　Let them find you not at home.
You've been given an expense paid vacation
　　From which, there's no need to return.

When pain and misery want to come and play,
　　Let them find an abandoned playground.
You have grown up and moved on
　　And now reside in another town.

Learn to seize the moment
　　And take advantage of opportunity.
Cast your bread, sow your seed, and
　　Live everyday with triumphant expectancy.

Celebrate your today
　　As if it is your tomorrow.
Don't let another day go by
　　Still living in yesterday's sorrow.

Embrace the possibilities
　　Your life has to offer.
This is my testimony!
　　This is how I got over!

Write a statement about yourself, relative to this poem, that you can begin to use to positively shape your thoughts and feelings.

_____

_____

_____

_____

"You can drive yourself crazy
trying to act normal!"

The Flip Side

What if you were born to be great?
   Wouldn't it be sad if you lived and died anything less?

What if you were born to be wealthy?
   Wouldn't it be tragic if you lived and died poor?

What if you were born to be a steward over many things?
   Wouldn't it be a travesty if you
      Lived and died a steward over nothing?

What if you were born to be a generous giver?
   Wouldn't it be pitiful if you
      Lived and died a treacherous borrower?

"What if" is a two-sided phrase.
   There is a side of fear and a side of faith.

Faith moves you to action.
   Fear traps you in paranoia.

If you live and walk in faith,
   You will become everything you're supposed to be.

But if you live and walk in fear,
   You will remain trapped
      On the flip side of "what if".

Write a statement about yourself, relative to this poem, that you can begin to use to positively shape your thoughts and feelings.

_____

_____

_____

_____

Failure Is No Excuse

If you can't remember anything else,
Remember this truth about yourself.

Say to yourself each day you arise,
I'm going to live because I'm alive!

I'm going to be because I am!
I'm going to do because I can!

I'm going to go because I'm willing!
I'm going to arrive because I'm not quitting!

No, I won't quit and say it's no use
Because I know that failure is no excuse!

I refuse to give up and I refuse to give in.
I refuse to go down or under again.

I have the spirit that cannot be conquered
And because of that I am always triumphant!

Write a statement about yourself, relative to this poem, that you can begin to use to positively shape your thoughts and feelings.

_____
_____
_____
_____

Wow Time

When the chips are down and the money is low,
  The bills are high and business is slow;

On the upside and on the real,
  You need something happening on an even keel.

Now is the time to use your imagination.
  Find a way to better your situation.

You have the power and you have the choice.
  You have the ability to sound your voice!

Creatively express your courage and class.
  Tap every reservoir and resource you have.

Do what it takes to get over the hump.
  You'll be glad you did when you reach triumph!

It's up to you and it's up to you now!
  Don't hold back! Make your life Wow!

Write a statement about yourself, relative to this poem, that you can begin to use to positively shape your thoughts and feelings.

_____

_____

_____

_____

Oh Butterfly

Oh butterfly, oh butterfly,
Who told you that you could not fly?

Where did you get the crazy idea
That the path for your life was not clear?

Why is it that you think
Hope has left you on the other side of the brink?

You need to know beyond any doubt
That the God of all has called you out.

He planned for you in love before the world began
To conform to His son's image as was His master plan.

So rise up, believe, open your heart, and receive.
Let your mind be free of all doubt and worry.

Fly, fly, high, high
Like the eagle in the sky!

Soar above and beyond
Your life's every norm.

Let the world see your splendor and beauty;
This is how it was meant to be.

Spread your wings and let your spirit go free.
Fulfill your purpose and reach your destiny!

Write a statement about yourself, relative to this poem, that you can begin to use to positively shape your thoughts and feelings.

_____

_____

_____

_____

Get up out of here
    You fear and doubt!
    I know who I am
And I am no slouch!

I'm a lean, mean, **The Commitment**
    Creating machine
    And I'm ready to take on
Whatever life brings!

I'm gonna tell the world
    What I'm all about.
    I'm gonna tell my story
Until it makes me shout!

You see, I have a purpose,
    A specific task.
    And I can't die
Until it comes to past!

So get out of my way negativity
    And move over complacency;

For I am committed to my destiny!

Write a statement about yourself, relative to this poem, that you can begin to use to positively shape your thoughts and feelings.

_____

_____

_____

_____

Contagious Infection

I won't be rattled by anything.
I've got the world in the palm of my hand.

I know who I am and where I'm going.
I know the reason why I'm sowing.

I sow my seed into the earth
Fully aware of its cost and its worth.

I sow my gift everyday
Knowing its coming back my way.

It's coming back greater than before,
Pressed down, shaken together, and running over-more.

I'll sow again and again and again
Because somebody is being blessed.
Somebody is being blessed
By the contagious infection of my success.

Write a statement about yourself, relative to this poem, that you can begin to use to positively shape your thoughts and feelings.

_____

_____

_____

_____

My Declaration

I, _____, do hereby solemnly declare that I will, from this day forward, do everything within my power to rid myself of every negative thought and energy that I have allowed to influence me in the past!

I realize that I have the power to do this!

I will win the battle to control my mind!

I have already won it!

I recognize that this battle is not against flesh and blood, but against principalities and powers whose mission is to enslave my mind!

Therefore, I will daily feed my mind with the positive necessary to combat the negative forces launched against me!

I, as an act of my own will, reverse the notion within me that it is easier to believe the negative than it is the positive!

I choose to believe the positive!

I choose to believe the truth about who I am!

I will diligently seek the truth about who I am, why I'm here, and what it is I'm to give before I leave!

I will find my true inner self!
I will embrace my true inner self!

I will become my true inner self!

I will fulfill, to its greatest extent, the purpose for which I came into this world!

Write a statement about yourself, relative to this piece, that you can begin to use to positively shape your thoughts and feelings.

_____

_____

_____

_____

Life has many hidden treasures

    For us to experience and enjoy.

        Sometimes they go unnoticed.

            Sometimes they are ignored.

                Sometimes we fail to see

The Greatest Treasure

                    Just how and where they fit

                    Into our busy schedules

              And lives we call complete.

            But, nevertheless, I say

        Love is the greatest treasure.

     Unconditional love indeed,

Of which, there is no measure!

Write a statement about yourself, relative to this poem, that you can begin to use to positively shape your thoughts and feelings.

_____

_____

_____

_____

A Father's Message To His Children

You can be anything
   That you want to be
  As long as you keep the faith
And never cease to believe.

You can conquer the world
   Or master the skies
    As long as you never forget
How to lift up your eyes.

You can change status quo
   Or how things are done
  As long as you remember
Where your help comes from.

You can invent, create,
   Initiate, and begin
    As long as you are committed to
Following through to the end.

You can reach for the stars
   And get them.
  Just make certain of what
You're rooted and grounded in.

You can discover, uncover,
   Reveal, and unveil
      As long as humility
Balances your scale.

You can do anything
   That you set your mind to
      In full assurance that
My spirit is with you.

I am your father!
   You are my children!
      We are one!
Nothing is impossible!

Write a statement about yourself, relative to this poem, that you can begin to use to positively shape your thoughts and feelings.

_____

_____

_____

_____

Today I Stand

Today **I stand**.

I stand for the under dog;
Those who've been counted out instead of counted in, Excluded instead of included,
Discouraged instead of encouraged,
Told that you would never make it, take it, or be able to shake it.

I stand for the down trodden;
The oppressed, depressed, and suppressed;
The people that don't have enough,
Aren't smart enough or pretty enough,
Aren't skinny enough or popular enough.

I stand for those who weren't supposed to be here;
Those who weren't supposed live;
Those who weren't supposed to dance, sing, speak, or walk.

I stand for those who got knocked down,
Pushed aside, walked on, and run over.

I stand for the illegitimate, unexcused, and misunderstood.

I stand for the looked over and outright disregarded.

I stand for the cast out, cast away, underrated, and unappreciated.
I stand because I have feet that are firmly planted on something I believe in.

I stand because I have legs that have not buckled under the pressures of life.

I stand because I have a heart that won't give up.

I stand because my arms are interlocked with others who also stand.

I stand because of my dream.

I stand because of the God who stands in me.

And so today **I stand**.

Write a statement about yourself, relative to this poem, that you can begin to use to positively shape your thoughts and feelings.

_____

_____

_____

_____

Destiny, The Final Order

When purpose and destiny have been revealed
And the promise on record has been fulfilled;

> When time has passed and run its race
> And every event has taken place;

> When love and life are fully expressed,
> Having endured all trials and tests;

> When the hoary head cannot be denied
> And legacy is seen in younger eyes;

When the heart has married wisdom
And the mind has embraced understanding;

Now is the time for the ultimate reward.

> The mission has been accomplished.
> His will has been done.

> The price has been paid.
> The race has been run.

> Lay down the gift. Pick up the crown.
> The final order has now come down!

Write a statement about yourself, relative to this poem, that you can begin to use to positively shape your thoughts and feelings.

_____

_____

_____

_____

What Happened To Hope?

The Truth is . . .
>Lost
>Values and morals sold at high cost
>Leaving destitute the future before us
>Paving the way to yet another spiritual holocaust

The Truth is . . .
>Gone
>That's why kids are left alone
>Trying to figure out this world on their own
>With no real guidance coming from home

The Truth is . . .
>We were destined to lose
>When they took prayer out of schools
>Now our kids are shooting, stabbing, acting like fools

The Truth is . . .
>They don't learn the right things in school
>They shun authority, discipline, and rules
>They kill for privileges that come with the silver spoon

The Truth is . . .
>We live in a world of deception
>Skewed by our misconception
>Twisted by our lack of perception

The Truth is . . .
>Our bodies crave things we don't need
>To medicate the pain that comes from the seed
>Of lies, fear, doubt, and negativity

The Truth is . . .

> Our families are all broken
> True confessions are still unspoken
> Lives destroyed are just a token

The Truth is . . .

> Time isn't on our side
> We can no longer afford to nurture the pride
> That keeps our feet stumbling and our hands tied.

The Truth is . . .

> It's not too late to turn it around
> Get our feet on solid ground
> Receive counsel that is proven to be sound

The Truth is . . .

> What holds this world together
> What keeps us loving each other
> What makes things get better

The Truth is . . .

> That hope we need
> To destroy the greed
> Preserve the seed
> And live like people freed.

"What God wants for you is what you want for you as long as what you want for you fall within the guidelines of what He wants for you and what He wants for you is much more than you could ever want for yourself!"

"No matter what happens to you in life and regardless of what someone says or does to you, you still have the controlling interest in what you think and how you respond."

The Motivational Poet

"How you handle scrutiny is a determining factor in your personal growth and development!"

"Don't get hoodwinked into believing a lie because you don't know the truth!
Find truth and stick to it!"

The Motivational Poet

"If you are waiting for tomorrow to come before you start doing something, I've got news for you:
Tomorrow will never come.
So you had better get busy today!"

"Life is not fair.
It's just what it is
And it is what *you* make it!"

"If you are to be happy with what tomorrow brings, then you must be content with what yesterday has laid to rest and occupied with what today offers!"

"No one else can do what you were born to do, like you were born to do it, when or where you were born to do it!"

The Motivational Poet

"You must have something to live for so that when you die, you don't die for nothing."

The Motivational Poet

"Winning is an attitude!

Failure is a decision to quit!

Your attitude determines your decision!"

The Motivational Poet

"Don't let the same problems cause you

To repeat the same patterns"

The Motivational Poet

An Excerpt from
The Psychology of a Dreamer

The Dreamer's Mentality:

1. **A dreamer becomes a dreamer when he acts on his dream!** Having a dream does not make you a dreamer. You must act on it.

2. **A dreamer flows in the creative! He is futuristic!** If the creative is not operative in your life, then your past will dominate your present and dictate your future.

3. **A dreamer has a firm sense of purpose!** He senses that the realization of his dream will have some lasting affect in life.

4. **A dreamer is hopelessly passionate!** This kind of passion is the ability and desire to get back up on the stage of life once you have been booed off.

5. **A dreamer will flourish in famine because of his dream and will cause other dreams to be birthed!** It is when things seem the worst that the dream is the clearest. This characteristic inspires other dreamers.

6. **Dreamers are hated by non-dreamers!** Dreamers are constant reminders to non-dreamers of what they could do, be, and have if they were not controlled by fear.

7. **Dreamers do not run from pain and adversity!** They embrace them and use them to accomplish their goals and objectives.

8. **A dreamer would rather die than settle for anything less than what he has seen behind his eyes!** A dreamer cannot bear the thought of, much less, see himself failing because he has already seen himself succeeding.

9. **A dreamer is not afraid to die, because he is not afraid to live!** He learns, through the process of pursuing his dream, how to seize life and its precious

moments of opportunity and he also learns the importance of the role death plays in life.

10. **When the dream is alive, a dreamer has as many lives as is necessary!** The giver of the dream gives life to the dreamer and the dream gives vitality to that life.

11. **A dreamer, at some point in time, recognizes his dream as a means to an end!** Your dream is what you were meant to accomplish. Your destiny is who you were meant to become. Your dream should speak of and point to your destiny. DON'T ALTER YOUR DESTINY TRYING TO REACH YOUR DREAM.

12. **A dreamer pursues his dream with integrity and respect for others!** He looks for ways to offer solutions, rather than create problems and always with the care, concern, and enhancement of others in mind.

Three Keys to Living Your Dreams, Fulfilling Your Purpose, and Reaching Your Destiny

In order to live your dreams, fulfill your purpose, and reach your destiny you must have three keys operating in your life. These keys are a part of a process we call Dominion Training Leadership and a model we call The Dream Factor. They have the ability to release you into your greatest levels of achievement and fulfillment. We would like to introduce you to these keys and encourage you to get the **Dominion Training Leadership Series** course or attend a seminar.

Key #1 is *Enhanced Awareness*, which involves sharpening your mind, focusing your will, and strengthening and understanding your emotions.

Key #2 is *Accurate Identity*, which involves recognizing your pattern or rhythm, distinguishing your voice, and identifying and clarifying your message.

Key #3 is *Absolute Direction*, which involves exposing your dreams, revealing your purpose, and unveiling your destiny.

Bibliography of Poems

All poems are written by Tim Jones, the Motivational Poet.

Other Products and Information

Books
Confessions of Faith: The Art of Renewing the Mind

CD's/Tapes/DVD's
The Indomitable Spirit
Why Do Kids Rebel?

Seminars/Workshops/Courses
The Dream Factor
Dominion Training Leadership
Why Do Kids Rebel

Dramas/Plays/Musicals
Apples of Gold
Rhythmology

For information on ordering other products and services or to request Tim Jones, the Motivational Poet as a speaker, please contact:

Motivational Poet
4147 White Heron Drive
Orlando, Fl 32808
mopoet@juno.com
www.motivationalpoet.com